Sense Your Way To

Life

Satisfaction

I0134702

Jo Anne White, Ph.D.

Copyright: 2007 by Jo Anne White, Ph.D.

This book is dedicated to my loving family wherein I was supported and encouraged to be me. For this, I am grateful. Thank you.

Warranty Disclaimer/Limits of Liability

This book is not intended to replace the services of a professional psychologist, counselor, or psychiatrist. It is intended for use by emotionally healthy persons with a desire to enhance their self-concept and personal achievement. The author and publishers make no warranty (expressed or implied) with respect to the suitability of this book for any particular personal situation of the user thereof. The author and publishers shall not be held liable for loss or any other damages including, but not limited to, special, consequential, incidental, or other damages. As always in the case of mental or emotional distress, seek the services of a competent professional.

Table of Contents

Prologue

I learned long ago how important our senses are to every experience that we have. And for over twenty years, I've taught others how to bring about more joy, success and satisfaction in their lives.

In this book, and in the Total Sense ® Life Success Programs and seminars that I developed in 1999, you are shown how to use your senses to create the life that you choose and the successes that you desire.

Your senses are your necessary and powerful allies to living your life with more awareness and conscious design. It's so wonderful when you discover how your senses are essential to your life creation. And more amazing, when you learn how to use them to your best advantage to attract what you want to you at any time.

This book gives you the basic principles that allow you to be the active creator of you and your life. These principles are invaluable to our understanding and acceptance, but not enough to show us the way. Exercises and activities are also included that have been used successfully in the Total Sense® Life Success Seminars and in private sessions with my clients. So the good news is that they have worked for thousands of others like you.

They can also work for you. You'll find out how to use your senses more consciously and prominently to bring about the successes that you desire in each area of your life.

You'll be Shown How to:
Be a Sensory Magnet
Increase your Passion
Magnify your Satisfaction
Amplify your Senses
Activate your Goals
Increase Self Appreciation
Change Defeating Thinking
Release Unwanted Memories and Habits

You can actively choose how and when your senses will be engaged in each life situation, and in your imagination, with ease and fun. Mastery of all eight senses, which includes your mind, can make your life and relationships more enriching. You'll feel more in charge; you'll be more empowered to bring into your life what you only previously imagined.

But just don't take my word for it. Like the thousands of other trailblazers before you, begin your journey to a more satisfying you. Blaze your own life trail right now. Your time is here.

There was a difficult time in my own life, following the death of my mother, when quite understandably my life was on automatic. I went about the motions of living with gray numbness. Creativity felt like something that had fled and that was so far out of my reach. As the grief began to lift, I listened to one of my own Total Sense® programs and followed the steps. What worked successfully in the past to stir the creative spark in my life, I again made a place for.

And that something was to turn on my senses and amplify them to feel and experience the most of everything, and to attend to what my senses were telling me.

I became aware of my breathing. Texture, color, taste, feeling, sound and thought were alive when I fully and consciously experienced each activity. It didn't matter if I was eating a tart and juicy blueberry, or stretching my limbs long and free. When my senses were enlivened, everything turned sharper, richer and more intense.

That is what this book offers and more. You will learn how to gain more control over your senses. You'll find out how to deepen sensory appreciation. By becoming a sensory magnet, you'll attract to you what you once thought impossible. You're invited to learn how to amplify what you already have or what is not yet present in your life.

You are now ready to tune into and amplify your senses to bring to you what you truly desire. I feel privileged to help you along the way.

I wish you many blessings, joys and successes.

Foremost, I wish you Love.

Please let me know how you're doing, I'd love to hear from you.

Jo Anne White, Ph.D.

Chapter One: Total Sensing

"When something is new to us, we treat it as an experience. We feel that our senses are awake and clear. We are alive."

Jasper Johns

Total Sense® Seminars

Inside are concepts from the Total Sense® Life Success Seminars and activities that I developed in 1999. There are also selections from *Making Sense*: *Pump up the Pleasure in your Life with Perception © White, 2004,* which is based on the principles and exercises from the Total Sense® Life Success Seminars held in North America.

You can use them immediately to make changes in your life and have more satisfaction. And you can design your life with conscious intention. Your senses will help you and so will your mind, which you'll learn, is just another sense that we have.

In all the Total Sense® Life Success Programs, you will gain skill and opportunities to move you in the direction you choose. These programs have one advantage in common. The Total Sense® Programs are designed to engage all your senses. All your senses are activated and that's what makes this method so special and effective.

The Total Sense® Life Success Programs have five core principles of life satisfaction. These are: Awareness, Charting Direction, Belief, Action and Union. Each of these steps will move you forward in your life to purposeful creation. Not only desiring something specific in your life, whether it's love or a new car, but knowing how to manifest it into reality is what we're all really after.

This book presents the underlying premises to the five steps: sensory engagement and sensory amplification. Simply put: we engage our senses and turn them up to produce the desired effect. With your senses turned on and tuned up, you can achieve more life satisfaction. We turn up our senses, consciously and willfully, to help us remember, repeat, change or newly create what we desire.

When your senses are fully and consciously engaged in whatever you do, something wonderful happens. You feel much better and you are more aware of everything. Your perception can change your experiences and make them conform to your wishes. Life is more satisfying. And it's possible to reach your limitless potential.

Just Imagine

Imagine living your limitless potential right now.

Imagine deepening the satisfaction that's already in your life.

And if satisfaction isn't there, imagine that you know how to put it back in your life. You can do it all with a simple conscious turn of an inner switch. You turn on and up your senses and Wow!

Your Eight Senses

That's right eight, and not the typical five senses that you're familiar with. Each of the eight senses plays an important role to achieve life satisfaction. You will find out how to use them more consciously and actively in your own life to get the results you want. Yes, I'm talking about outcomes, but I also believe that the process to reach those outcomes is important too. Your process doesn't have to be strenuous and boring. Instead, you can have enjoyment and expectant energy along the way to those outcomes. Imagine the path to your life satisfaction being as much fun and as stimulating as your arrival.

In the Total Sense® Life Success Programs, we use all eight major senses. You already know of sight, hearing taste, smell and touch. You use these senses all the time whether or not you've been aware of what they're recording or attending to. You may not rely on your sixth sense right now. Perhaps you don't believe it can accurately influence your decisions and your life, yet it can.

Sixth Sense:

Many people refer to the sixth sense as the psychic sense or extrasensory perception (ESP). When this sense is turned on, we get all sorts of information in the form of impressions, feelings, dreams, hunches, premonitions, thoughts and maybe even visions. Not everyone's use of their intuitive sense is well-seasoned or developed, but it can be. The intuitive sense can serve as an additional instrument for your use. Intuition can aid you in making accurate decisions and creating more satisfaction.

If you admit it to yourself, you've had moments when you relied on, or didn't pay attention to your intuition or your sixth sense. Maybe it paid off, or maybe you wished you had listened to the advice. In this book, you'll learn new ways to use your sixth sense that will supplement the other seven senses and add meaning.

Seventh Sense: Your Mind

There is another sense that you're familiar with. You may not consider the mind a sense although it is. Your mind is called the seventh and master sense by the yogis because without it your other senses would not function. With the mind in gear, we can perceive the outside world and make sense of it. We can also perceive and interpret our internal world.

When we are in control of the mind, the mindless chatter that goes on, often under our radar, is quieted. We all know how those unwanted thoughts can be irritating. Sometimes, they interfere with what we're doing. They can defy us and even hold us back. Yet, when we consciously use the mind, our master sense, it is alert and awakened to countless messages. When we recognize and follow these messages, we can enrich our experiences.

The yogis also believe that we must go beyond the mind and beyond the other senses. We do this to attain a greater understanding of the vastness of the universe and of ourselves. This happens only after we have experienced the senses as fully as we possibly can. Once we are aware of their depth and what knowledge and joy they bring to us, we are ready to empty ourselves of them. We enter the void and the stillness where we can discover a deeper sense of joy and being. We move beyond the senses, into a state of what yogis call Pratyahara or sense withdrawal. Here, we stop identifying with the limitations of the body, the personality and the mind, so that we can see beyond them and transcend them.

Eighth Sense: Propriception:

The eighth sense, known as pro*prioception,* is one that we're not always conscious of. With it, we learn about the location, posture and movement of our bodies. Without it, we might bump into walls and into each other all the time. And we'd fumble around uncertainly with inaccurate perception of how we are in the world. With proprioception, we can feel and identify with our bodies and we also receive feedback about them. If this sense didn't function properly, we wouldn't be able to sense our own bodies. Imagine feeling disembodied and cut off from your body, lost to where you are in space. Lost to where you begin and end. What would walking, driving, eating or expressing yourself feel like?

Activate Your Senses

As you read this book and complete the suggested exercises, you'll awaken and amplify all eight of these senses. Be ready to reap success from these activities. Be prepared to engage in new ways of thinking that will permanently increase the amount of love, success and satisfaction you experience. Throughout this book are specific activities designed to help you wake up and expand your senses so that you can dramatically influence your internal and external worlds.

You'll activate the energy and awareness centers in your body. By doing so, you will participate more fully in life and experience the world more profoundly. Your ability to access and amplify your senses holds the key to a more exciting, enjoyable and rewarding life.

When your perception is consciously changed and your senses bring you the information and understanding you need, your life will not only feel, but *be* matched to your own specifications of joy and meaning. What once was difficult now not only seems, but *is* easier. And, you are creating more energy, more living and loving than you once thought possible.

In this book and in the Total Sense® Life Success Seminars, we consciously pay attention to our senses; we turn them up to amplify them. This makes the incoming sensory information more potent and easier to remember and recall.

We use our senses to our advantage to consciously create what we choose in our lives. All the successes and feelings of satisfaction that we project are enhanced by how we use our senses. This book is your gateway to them.

Chapter Two: Sense Appeal

"The moment one gives close attention to anything, even a blade of grass, it becomes a mysterious, awesome and magnificent world in itself. "

Henry Miller

Sense Power

Our senses are powerful. They connect us to the world and to others. Because of our senses, we receive data all the time about what is taking place outside of us. They also tell us about what's happening inside of us. With your senses, you can experience greater appreciation and understanding. That is, when you pay attention. At those moments, your perception is on full alert.

When this happens, your brain is very active, more than it was before. It makes new neural pathways. And this is where it gets exciting. All these new pathways in your brain increase your thinking power.

Your creativity is also turned up. New ideas and associations come to you more easily. Your perception is clearer. You may even perceive differently than before. With new insight and with your eight senses, you will learn how to perceive and sense differently. And you can willfully create more positive experiences in your life. With your senses in gear, these experiences can stay with you throughout your life. And you will be able to create more favorable experiences all the time.

Genius Mind

After Albert Einstein's death and with his family's permission, scientists removed his brain from his head for study and research. What was inside his noggin that made such a genius, researchers pondered? Is a genius's gray matter any different from yours or mine? And if so, how was his unique?

Once they dissected his brain, scientists found an unusual amount of glial cells. Glial cells are traditionally considered the "housekeeper cells" of the brain. They clean up debris in the brain. They also provide physical and nutritional support for the neurons, which transfer electrical signals and shape our thoughts, dreams and images.

New research suggests that these glial cells participate in processing information by actively influencing, and maybe even controlling the activity of the neurons. They help neurons sculpt circuits that are crucial to thinking and making novel associations. Novel associations lead to novel thinking and creation that may be astounding. As we learn more, additional neural connections and pathways are formed in our brain increasing our brain power and creativity.

The presence of so many glial cells also suggests that Einstein's scientific method did not rely on logic alone. He trusted his senses, intuition, imagination and feelings as important sources for his inquiry. Just as you are learning to do, which, without a doubt can have the same impact. The more you learn and rely on not just logic, but imagination, sensing and intuition, the more connections and new pathways can be created in your brain. When this happens, you too can have the makings of a genius mind.

We Are Energy

Do you know that all of your feelings, thoughts, and beliefs carry energy? They are like magnets of attraction and pull in more of whatever you send out.

And so are you! Energy, that is. And because you are, you can do amazing things. You're not as solid as you think you are. And you're not stuck in one state or way of being forever.

Instead, each one of us is made up of more than ninety-nine percent energy. This means our bodies are constantly changing with the natural capacity to make ourselves over and be different. We can tap into energy's essential nature to move and change and be transformed into new possibilities or potentialities.

Since we, too, are made of that energy, we also have that same infinite potential. Not only that, we can shift our reality with a mere thought, a feeling and an intention. Your choices and perception can really change how things are. They can even change how you are.

Shift Your Reality

Impossible, you say? Don't just take my word for it. Take the views and research findings of quantum physicists. They'll tell you that reality is not fixed and can be changed. And what's more amazing is that reality really is in the eye of the beholder.

Not just with your eyes, but with all your senses in gear, you have the ability to do astounding feats. You have the ability to change your world. That's where your senses come in. It all happens with perception. How you perceive what is taking place both outside and inside you can have more of an impact on what's happening than you ever realized.

With understanding, new awareness and the use of your senses, you can send out different energy than you have before. You decide what energy you want to send out and what energy you want to come back to you. And you also decide what form it will take.

21

The Relationship between Science and Spirit

Scientists, such as mechanic and quantum physicists, are now discovering what religions have been teaching for millennia. They now understand that some kind of universal, life-force energy flows between all objects and beings with intelligence, purpose and unity. Our brain receives every bit of information it processes, including our memories, through its interaction with this field.

The presence of this unified field means that boundaries between us and other people are not as defined as we think. As the mom who senses over the distance that something is wrong with her child, no separation exists between our selves and our environment, or between one person and another. We are truly connected. The life-force energy that flows through all things is akin to the Holy Spirit.

You Are In Charge

Quantum physics also tells us that each of us has a lot more control over the circumstances of our lives than we may be aware of. We now understand that objects and matter take form based upon how we focus on and see them.

Scientists now know that even so-called solid objects, like a chair or a brick or a wall, only appear to be solid because that's how the mind interprets them. On a sub-atomic level, the chair is composed almost entirely of empty space, no matter how solid it appears to the naked eye. The same is true with the way we've designed our life; it's more flexible than we may be aware. These ideas may sound radical, or like science fiction to you. But, the nature of the chair—the way it looks and how its molecules are organized to create it—are influenced by us, the observers.

The existence of the chair and our world is dependent upon our experience of each. This is why one person may call a blue-green car blue and another may label it green. Each experience is subjective. The observer is partially responsible for what is created.

We are not merely observers; we shape what's out there in the world at the same time that we view it.

Like a self-fulfilling prophecy, how we view our bodies, our jobs and our relationships affects both how they look and what they will look like in the future.

So when we form our impressions about what's "out there" based on what we are seeing, it's as if we've taken a photograph of what we believe we see. This freezes the scene in our minds. It also creates something like a fixative solution that solidifies the object in physical form.

Thus, we have some say—some control—over how our world is designed. What this can mean is that the way we see the world is responsible for forming and shaping our experiences. This flow of messages back and forth from the brain to the body contributes not only to how we feel at this very moment, but how we will feel at a later date. Taken one step further, it suggests that the way we see the world is responsible for forming and shaping our experiences.

Meet Maxine, a 54-year-old accountant. She's angry with her husband Sam for not leaving her a decent dinner after she works very late one night during tax season. Maxine

24

always sets aside a plate for him and she expects that he will reciprocate. Sam is already asleep when she gets home, so Max stews. Angry thoughts mount as she creates an argument in her head. Instead of getting a good night's sleep, she fumes and steams. When Sam says "good morning" she lights into him. He realizes he made a mistake, so the argument is brief. Sam apologizes and they work it out. Life is calm again and Maxine regains her composure.

Later in the week while driving home from work in rush hour, another driver rams the back end of her car. "Crunch!" Now Maxine's bumper is squashed and her rear light signal is knocked out. Coincidence? No, not really. Maxine may not realize that the minor car accident that delays her another forty-five minutes and will raise her insurance rates is related to her earlier moments of raging anger.

Quantum physics tells us that the angry energy Maxine was feeling and thinking was sent out into the universe. That anger she worked up pulled into her an event—in this case a car accident—that carried with it a similar vibration. The events are connected by the Law of Attraction, which I'll review below. It may be hard to believe right now. I encourage you to first test the idea before you ignore the information and throw it out.

What Messages Are You Sending?

So when we're feeling lousy we have to change the feelings and messages we're feeding ourselves. Otherwise, we'll continue sending out lousy vibrations that will come back to haunt us later in the form of unwanted experiences. While this information may seem daunting, it's important and empowering to know that we are in control of what happens to us. By changing how and what we think about now, we can affect our health and our future. Amazingly, our lives are wide open and we can tap into and create the billions of possibilities out there. This reality offers us hope.

How amazing it is to think that we are true creators even down to matter and the cellular level! Knowing this, imagine what you can do. Consider how much influence you can have on most things in your life. And when stuff is going wrong, maybe it's just because our attention has been on the negative. And, we've attracted what we *don't* want to happen rather than focusing on attracting the positive, or what we *do* want to happen.

The Law of Attraction

There are many natural Universal Laws, such as the Law of Gravity, which describe basic principles about how life and the universe work. They don't rule us. Yet like gravity, we are subject to them whether or not we're aware of their existence. The Law of Attraction is one such law.

Lately, there has been a lot of attention to the Law of Attraction and how people can use it to their benefit. I like to believe that it's also used to help make the world a better place. I'm really excited about the possibilities as more people catch on to how this law works because of what I believe is its great creative potential.   I've been successfully using this law in my own life for over twenty years, while also teaching my students, clients and seminar participants to do the same. They've learned how the law works with proven techniques that they can use to assist them in making it all happen.

Consciously working with it can have profound results for you too. Knowledge and understanding of this law have been around for a long time and effectively used by many people including successful writers, artists, business men and women to better their lives.

The Law of Attraction determines the kind of energy we attract to ourselves right now and in the future. Our emotions and the thoughts we think carry creative energies. Pleasant feelings and thoughts such as love and joy pulsate at a high frequency, or vibration. They affect our brain and stomach centers to release chemicals such as neuropeptides that increase feelings of ease and wellness. The more the chemicals are produced in our brains, the better we feel.

Depression, jealousy and anger carry with them vibrations that create the corresponding "negative" feelings in our cells. Are they really negative? No, but they don't satisfy us the way loving thoughts do. They don't release any feel-good hormones and we feel that, too. Missing is the emotional lift in us that we experienced earlier with the other energies like compassion and love.

The Law of Attraction states that people, matter and circumstances are drawn to similar energetic vibrations. Like magnets, we attract more of the same energy that we're already giving off.

So what does it mean that our thoughts and feelings vibrate to different frequencies? We are always drawing to us more of what we're thinking and feeling. The people and situations in our life come to us because of how we are and because of what we focus on. The good news is that now that we're aware, we can actively do something about it. Not only do we know what we're attracting, we plan on it and make it so.

The Law of Attraction in Nature

Nature provides many powerful examples of the Law of Attraction in action. The vibration of nectar attracts bees and insects. This is nature's way of helping flowers and plants pollinate and keep their species alive. Bees and insects, which play an essential role, are seduced by the nectar's vibration and land on the flower and feed. When they are satisfied they fly away, taking the seeds of the next generation with them.

While flower nectar is irresistible to butterflies and bees, elephants, polar bears and fish literally aren't "on the same wavelength" and, therefore, aren't drawn to them.

Similar to the attracting power of flower nectar, your feelings, thoughts and beliefs are also magnets of attraction. They pull in more energy similar to whatever energy you send out. Yet, while this makes sense to us when we look at the outside world, it can be difficult to grasp when we apply it to our own lives.

Take Credit

Most people are willing to take credit for the hard work that landed them a promotion. But when events don't go right, they are accustomed to blaming their bosses, spouses and anything else, rather than identifying the ways in which they're responsible. No matter how much we may want to argue that we're not at fault or to blame, our argument doesn't make a difference. The Law of Attraction doesn't have anything to do with fault or blame. Like the Law of Gravity, it just is.

You Choose

You can't deny what you now know. Your thoughts, beliefs and actions determine what the outcomes are in your life. Now is the time to change them. When you do, the outcomes will change too. At first you pay attention. You figure out what you've been telling yourself and believing all these years, or at least right now. And, you decide to do something different.

You choose new thoughts to replace the worn-out ones. They haven't brought all that you've needed. These new thoughts can bring about different emotions. Your beliefs also change. What first began as imaginative feeling and belief becomes real.

> **You have the power to change your thoughts and your emotions right now!**

Your senses play a vital role in how you feel, think, act and how you connect to other people. You can learn to use them more fully for your positive advantage.

Conscious Creation at Work

When we decide to work consciously with the Law of Attraction, we can learn how to lasso in exactly what we desire in life. We become clearer about our goals. As we tune into and turn up our senses, we send out vibrations that we've already reached our goal, causing it to speed toward us.

The more sensory detail and upbeat feeling we can consciously create and associate with a particular goal, the easier we can attract our goal. Understanding how to use energy and our vibration in this way helps us become magnets. When we do, we create new energy patterns in our selves and in our world that attract our goals and dreams.

Your imagination is very active and helps you create the feelings and the sensory detail. Use the following Goal Getter Activity for each goal that you set. Create enthusiasm and excitement for each one of your goals. Believe and trust that it's on the way to you. The more you make it believable and the more you are convincing to you, the likelihood of reaching that goal in your life increases.

You can bring into your life what you choose and desire. It happens by recognizing the power of the Law of Attraction for you. You realize the power and influence that you really can have in your own life. You can begin right at this moment and influence the next moment, and the next.

Maybe it's not a new concept for you and maybe you've heard about it before, but you weren't wholeheartedly convinced. You may not be totally convinced now and that's fine. All you need to do is follow the steps. For a while, just allow your creative imagination and excitement to make believe. You need to believe that it's possible. Believe that you're pulling your desires in with a giant force with your mind and feelings right now and, of course, with your senses.

Activity 1: Goal Getter

1. Choose a goal that you would like to bring into your life.

2. Write it down.

3. Write down how you'll feel when that goal has arrived.

4. Conjure up an image(s) of having your goal both in your mind and on paper.

5. Play the images over and over in your mind.

6. Play the feelings of joy and excitement derived from reaching your goal right now.

7. Turn on and turn up your senses for each goal.

8. Include as much sensory detail in your images as possible.

9. Include sense feelings for each goal experience.

Chapter Three: Sensory Awareness

"There is no way in which to understand the world without first detecting it through the radar–net of our senses."

   Diane Ackerman

Fields of Awareness

Our senses are fields of awareness. Each one gives us detailed and unique messages all the time. With our senses, we figure out what the environment around us is like. We also learn how to respond to it physically, physiologically and emotionally. Not only are we informed through our senses, they make the environment and our experiences fuller and more animated. Pleasure can increase, as well as pain.

Sensory awareness is self-awareness. We interact all the time with our world. Our senses optimize our experiences. How we are in the world can be just for survival, or can be for the wonder and delight in being alive.

When we ignore vital sensory information, we risk being on automatic pilot. Our tasks, our lives and maybe even our relationships become habitual. And our responses are automatic.

Sensory Response

With Sensory Awareness, you connect more fully to your body, your humanness and the physical world. And you connect more fully to all the experiences that are in it.

After you've learned how to consciously amplify and respond more with your senses, you can more comfortably learn to shut down the external stimulation. Then you can pay attention to the internal and to the quiet within. You become easy with the silence and understand its gifts.

Sensory Awareness practices pave the way for yoga meditation. To move past the senses and the external world in meditation, attention is turned inward to the breath, the body, the mind and then beyond. When we let go of the world and the senses, mind and body, we enter a place of stillness. Within the silence, we experience higher consciousness.

By letting in the information from our senses, the world's a livelier place, more colorful and more responsive.

Spend Time with Your Senses

How can we appreciate what our senses reveal to us?

Spend some conscious time, an hour, a few hours or even a day. Become aware of as much sensory information as possible. Just be with the stimuli that come in, without your mind and without labels. Just Experience…

Thoughts and words get in the way of your experience, and distance you from appreciating them.

To appreciate more, you need to be quiet. Turn off thoughts that distract you from the moment. Let go of worrying about the past that's already happened and the future that you can now change with the tools you are being given. Worry won't change anything and will clutter up your mind. Instead, become absorbed and engaged in the specific experience of the moment. Pay attention to what the senses are offering you in the way of feelings, information and detail.

This is sense appreciation and can lead you to a heightened awareness of yourself and your world. A feeling of aliveness and discovery can return to you. Any action, from cooking to walking, can be an opportunity for the awareness of your direct experience. Release the habit in each activity so that you don't take each experience for granted.

Awaken your senses and know the richness of the sensory world.

Activity 2A: Sense Alert

❖   Do these exercises without words. Be an
    observer and explorer.

❖   Tune into each sense and just attend to what
    you receive through sight, touch, smell, taste
    and hearing.

❖   Pay attention to how things feel; take in the
    texture of objects.

❖   Be alert to the incoming smells from your
    environment.

❖   Spend moments just slowly, slowly tasting a
    piece of fruit, an almond or anything. Feel it,
    smell it, allow it into your senses. Fill your
    senses with the scent of it and the sound of it
    as you eat it.

41

❖   Take some time to experience your food with your eyes and sense of smell. If it's a finger food, experience it between your fingers.

❖   Now imagine yourself taking small bites, feeling it in your mouth, taste it slowly taking it in, chewing slowly and consciously.

❖   Feeling the texture in your mouth and the shape of it changing as you chew it and it melts. Really experience the warmth, the flavor, the texture when it is in your mouth.

❖   Let your tongue fully experience the sweetness or saltiness. Feel how good it makes the inside of your mouth and tongue feel.

❖   Engage yourself in another activity and another. With each activity, see how many senses you can consciously pull into the experience.

Activity 2B: Isolate Your Sense

- ❖ Spend some time with just one of your senses like touch or smell and only attend to the stimuli for that sense alone.

- ❖ For example, with your sense of hearing, listen to the variations of sounds in your world and to the sounds that take place when you work or perform a task like sweeping or surfing the internet.

- ❖ Listen to the natural sounds and sounds that occur at different times of the day.

- ❖ Now move on to another sense. Be totally present with each sense experience.

❖ It's important to only concentrate as fully as possible on one sense at a time. Don't be discouraged. You will learn to tune out the other senses so that you fully take in the experience of one sense at a time.

❖ Don't rush being with your one sense. The more you linger, the more you'll discover and the more you'll be aware of.

❖ Take the time to do these activities and experience more depth to the commonplace and more joy in each moment.

Chapter Four:
Habits - Understanding and Release

"The real voyage of discovery consists of not in seeking new landscapes but in having new eyes."

Leonardo Da Vinci

Habit Takeovers

The body's natural and optimal state of being and functioning is one of wholeness and balance. In living day to day, we often lose sight of this. We unconsciously develop distorted ways of thinking and moving that become habits. Sometimes our habits take over until we mistakenly believe they are "right", or simply "the way things are."

Habits are learned behaviors or actions, such as shoe tying, practiced over and over zillions of times. They become mechanical ways we relate to our environment and to ourselves.

With repetition, the habit becomes so ingrained that we don't even think about what we're doing. We don't have to think. We perform the task automatically. Over time, these behavioral patterns become unconscious. We do them easily without thinking because they've become second nature to us.

The Importance of Habits

Although they become automatic, habits are important. Imagine if every time you tied your shoe, you had to think about what was involved in the actual lacing. What if you had to do that for all the other simple tasks that you perform thousands of times—tasks like walking, washing or opening you door latch with a key?

If you hadn't learned to do it by rote, every single time you performed that activity, you would have to stop and think about each detail. Your mind would be so bogged down by remembering the simpler tasks that you wouldn't be able to do anything else. Forget about multi-tasking.

Repetitive patterns can be physical, emotional and mental habits. When our habits take over, our thoughts, movement and behaviors slip into familiar and worn paths.

We have to get past the habitual use of our senses so that we can respond differently and more creatively.

When Habits Get in Your Way

The risk of doing things unconsciously is that we become prisoners to our own faulty or outdated feeling, thinking and behaving. Habits can distort our perception and behavior. The roads they lead us down are not always accurate, even though we may think our path is "right."

We can get so comfortable and used to doing something, like slumping in our chairs, that our bodies get accustomed to being in that position. When that happens, we mistakenly believe that it's "normal." Once we find out slouching puts more stress on the lower back and spine and creates more fatigue, we still struggle to let go. It's difficult to get out of the habit even when we want to. Habits can be harmful. They may lead to even more stress in other parts of our bodies.

For many of us, "wrong" has become "right" and is ingrained in our actions, movements and sense-feelings. Because of the hold habits have on us, it's almost impossible to change our experiences. We must make a conscious effort to reorganize our ways of feeling, thinking and being. Unfortunately, we may not recall anything different. Balance, and the way we experience us in space and action, can be compromised.

Even when our habits create more misaligned posture, stress or stagnant thinking, few of us know how to release them. As a result, we get stuck in set ways of thinking, feeling and being that no longer work for us.

Unconscious habits contribute to our misuse of our body and mind. They are not separate but unified. They influence each other as well as have a role in how we feel. A conscious understanding of how we use the body and mind helps us to analyze and transform our lives. When we're consciously aware, our body and mind are affected by the sensory information we process and interpret.

Automatic Response

When we are stuck in outdated habits, we don't experience new sensations and feeling. Numbness and addiction can set in. Our ability to use and appreciate our senses gets out of whack.

We've all had the experience of walking or driving someplace on "automatic pilot" and not remembering how we arrived at our destination. On automatic pilot, our senses are dulled and we don't pay attention to what's around us. We are in motion and going somewhere and that's all that matters. Yet, we are numb to the beautiful gold and red palate of autumn leaves, the joyful sounds of children laughing, the scent of our car's air freshener. No wonder we don't enjoy the experience.

Habit Makeovers

The good news is we can change our emotional, physical and mental responses. Even the worn-out habits we've been unaware of will change. Through re-education and sensory training, we can recover our ability to create free movement and choices in our lives. Conscious understanding of how we use the body and mind helps us to transform our lives.

To make this transition isn't demanding and is easier than you think, but it does take practice. Practice being alive and being conscious with your senses fully turned on to restore *psycho-physical equilibrium,* or mind-body balance. The rewards of having your senses at their peak are many.

By being conscious with your senses, you'll experience freedom that leads to creative thinking and action. The body, mind, emotions and all senses are alive and able to receive information differently and also act on that information in a novel way.

Think of moments and experiences that you've had that were enriched because your senses filled you up with all kinds of pleasurable information. Information you wanted to remember, and perhaps linger over because you felt good when you did.

Be aware when you shut down your sensations. Do you recall a time when you walked somewhere and didn't even notice your surroundings? Three blocks, ten blocks? And because your senses were shut off, you remember nothing about the experience. You were somewhere else. Blind, deaf and oblivious to the present, you were in the past, in the future and in your thoughts.

Sometimes it's fine to be oblivious to the sensory experiences because we're concentrating and attending to something else, something more important at the time. At these times, we need to turn-off the sensory stimulation. Just be aware that you're doing so. Know when that happens. And when you're ready, remember to turn them back on.

> **When we let go of our habits and learn new ways of conscious reasoning, we are able to create new ways of being and doing.**

Return to your Senses

At other times, shutting down is being on automatic pilot, or in our heads and our thoughts rather than participating in the present moment. When we do this, we miss out on what's happening and we lose touch with what is truly around us. When you notice this taking place, return to your senses. Rather than getting stuck in your thoughts or daydreaming, remind yourself to consciously pay attention to what's going on around you and in you. Do this by focusing on your senses. When you do, you'll learn to be in the present of each wondrous alive moment.

Activity 3: Habit Release

Before you can change a habit, you have to know it's there.
Only then can you do something about it.

Do It:

✱   For one, two, three hours, for a full day, or for as long
    as you like, practice doing things differently.

✱   Start out walking with the foot that you don't always
    use or write with your other hand. How do you feel?

✱   Notice how you feel in space. Become aware of how
    you move and your relationship to your surroundings.
    Close your eyes and feel the difference.

✱   Notice when you go on automatic pilot. Stop and do
    the next action and be very present with it.

✱   Notice how you feel when you're paying attention.
    What senses were turned on in the conscious activity?

Use your senses a new way too.

Can you:

Listen with your hands

Taste with your eyes

See with your body

Touch with your mouth

Speak with no words

Feel with your ears

Laugh with your eyes

Sense with your mind

Walk without sound

Let tastes explode, visions warm your skin, sounds deepen your feelings.

Chapter Five: Sensory Journey

"How does your experience of one sense affect all the others? In addition to being the conduits of pleasure and pain, your senses are the midwives of intelligence."

Michael J. Gelb

Sensory History

The senses have always been our way into the understanding of our world, and our lives.

Our senses have been the road to discovery since we've been very young.

Whether or not we've been conscious of them or used the information they've given us, we have been on a sensory journey since even before birth. In our mother's womb, we were aware of the warm temperature, of the rocking movement, of whooshing sound, of mother-smells and textures.

We emerged into the world as babes that rely foremost on what our senses tell us. We recognized our mother through her sweet smell, gentle touch, cooing voice, the feel of her face against ours, the sensation of milk flowing from her breast.

As toddlers, the world brought new sensory experiences. We explored our surroundings, played with toys and learned about other people and ourselves by heat or cold, by the tone and timbre of voices. We learned that the sounds of airplanes and trains were different. The look and feel of objects, from crayons to woolen gloves, weren't the same. They had different textures and uses. During childhood, we begin to understand, piece together and organize our world and the objects and people in it. We do that by using our senses, language and information from those who influenced us.

As adults, our experiences are so much richer as well because of our senses. A father's sensory memories of the three pound fish his ten-year old son caught are more vivid. Why? Because of the sense information that was present at the time. The fishy smell and how slippery the fish felt as it wiggled while his son shouted excitedly, all help him recall a 10-year-old family vacation.

Sensory Clues

For our entire lives, our senses have assisted us in the understanding of our world, our lives. They have guided us, helped us navigate the known and unknown and brought us countless messages. Our world and our sense of where we are take on more meaning and richness because of them. We formulate our ideas, perceptions and ways of acting and participating in the world based on these innate abilities.

It is with the senses that our memories linger long after the experience is gone. Whether the memory is a positive or negative one, it has been distilled, recorded with the smells, tastes, sights, sounds, feelings, thoughts and impressions of our existence.

So how do we alter the negative responses to situations that tug at us and pull us into a powerful web of remembering? Again, it's with our senses.

Sensory Memories

Sensory Memories are very powerful and can be recreated quickly and spontaneously. For example, imagine that you are walking past a bakery. The strong scent of cinnamon reaches your nostrils and you are suddenly taken all the way back to a warm and fuzzy childhood memory.

You remember helping your grandmother in the kitchen as she made cookies. Instantly, you feel warm and comfortable just like you did twenty or so years before. What happened? The cinnamon smell was associated with good feelings of acceptance and love and stored in your brain. At the moment that the familiar scent was picked up, the memory resurfaced, and so did the good feeling attached to the early memory.

You may find this hard to swallow, but I believe that it's also possible to change old sense memories and create new ones alongside of the old. We change our sense memories, consciously creating new ones that fit into our new schema of how things are. Unpleasant memories can be changed when we switch off the old sensory stimuli and create new sense awareness and information. I realize how radical this seems, but it can be effective. I know, because I've used it countless times in private sessions with dramatic results for my clients. Here's what happens. The new more pleasant memories and sense experiences become a part of the past memories and become associated with them. They buffer the unpleasant former memories we have. They add something more palatable to these old memories, diminishing their power and unpleasantness.

Sense Anew

New sense appeal offers us a different way of viewing old events. The sensory ties that have bound us to our anger, doubt, feelings of abandonment or a loveless past can be cut and we are free. Free to create new sensory information that delight, engage, and change our perceptions of how it was — all with a new sensory map. What this means is that we begin to sense a former experience differently than before. This can change the emotional impact of the experience. How we view it in our minds can also change.

It's truly like sensing anew and releasing ties we no longer want to be linked to.

Sensory Recording

We record information through our senses every moment and for just an instant, the information is stored in the brain. Even when you're not fully paying attention to what your ears, eyes or other senses are taking in, it happens anyway.

You may not be aware of the information as it's recorded; in a few fleeting seconds, your senses tune into something else. Most of the sensory information we get doesn't stay with us. After a few seconds, this information leaves our short-term memory.

Every experience we have passes through filters and is weeded out based on our need or desire to know or not know. Our filters decide which information is interesting or valuable enough to grasp onto for a short while. Otherwise, it's thrown out.

Smell blasts our memory like no other sense.

Your skin is the largest receiver of sensory information. Your emotions can be detected by touch. Anger and contentment are accompanied by physical sensation like tingling or tension in the skin or deep muscles.

Life has richness and meaning through our senses. The clean, soft smell of a baby, the tender and lingering touch of a lover, the spontaneous lilting laughter of a friend, the taste of our favorite chocolate dessert are all lasting memories.

Sensory Recall

We can conjure up our memories and recall them without even trying because of the sensory information linked to them. Sometimes we are bombarded with sense impressions—a waterfall of smells, a symphony of tastes.

Our senses tell us we are safe. They alert us to danger. We feel at home with them, or, as a ship adrift at sea.

So why not use them to your best advantage and consciously turn them up and pay attention to the messages, building the life that you choose?

Activity 4: Memory Jogging

1. **Think about a memory (a minor disappointment) that you wish had turned out differently.**

2. **Recall as much sensory information as you can.**

3. **Think about how you would have liked it to turn out, if you could do it over.**

4. **Pretend you can do it over.**

5. **This time make the action, sense information and your feelings all reflect this positive outcome that you envision.**

6. **Play it over and over in your mind and feelings.**

Remember now's not the time to conjure up deep-seated emotional pain. If you need to do so and need to speak with someone about it, please seek professional help!

Chapter Six: Sensory Awakening

"The moment one gives close attention to anything, even a blade of grass, it becomes a mysterious, awesome and magnificent world in itself".

Henry Miller

Become Self Aware

Becoming more self-aware is about paying attention to where you are and how you feel in each moment in time. It means to be more conscious of internal thoughts and feelings, as well as the external surroundings and experiences.

You make a commitment to be "present" in your life and body and choose not to sleepwalk through life. Whatever happens in your life, you realize is your responsibility. You are aware of what you are feeling, experiencing and even thinking, whether grief-stricken, angry or joyful.

We are aware of the difference between how, for example, resentment and compassion feel in our bodies. And we recognize the interrelationship among our thoughts, emotions and physical well-being. Being present is to know as best we can what's happening in us and outside of us.

Fortunately, the senses we already have offer an important gateway to greater self-awareness.

Sensory Shut Down

Yet at some point in life, many of us begin to gloss over sensory information and begin habitually going about our tasks and our lives with numbness. Sometimes this happens when we are busy, active or stressed. We take for granted a lot of what's going on and allow our responses to become automatic.

Sensations and emotions also can also be deadened through trauma or injury. We may find ourselves feeling bound to *sensory memories*—memories of experiences that we recall because our senses were heightened and engaged at the time—that stir up anger, doubt, feelings of abandonment or a loveless past, for instance.

The memory remains even if we feel it's lost to us. The sensory information from that incident is also strong and very vivid. Very suddenly, we can be pulled into the incident if we are reminded of, for example, a scent or sound. Any strong sensory information from that time can conjure up the memory for us. It doesn't really matter if the memory is pleasurable or not.

Stay Tuned to Your Senses

When we shut down our sensory awareness, we become less conscious of what our senses are telling us and then lose touch with our bodies and our lives. We stop experiencing the full spectrum of sensations. As a result, we may miss or filter out subtle, yet vital sensory information and stimuli. We also miss out on how they could help us change our minds and shift our actions in ways that would give us more enjoyment.

For example, have you ever been so consumed with worry while eating, say, a turkey sandwich or an apple that afterward you had no recollection of what your food tasted like? Or, been so busy thinking or being in your head that you didn't notice the colorful flower garden right in front of you?

When we spend time dissecting and doubting our past actions and decisions or worrying about the future, we get stuck. Automatic patterns of thinking, moving and being compromise how we relate to our selves, others and the world. We set ourselves up to experience tension. A person who is upset can unknowingly tense up all the muscles in her neck and back and hiking up her shoulders. This tension causes unwanted physical discomfort or even pain.

Thankfully, we can move past our preconceived responses and habitual uses of our senses. Instead, we can draw directly from the raw material they provide us and respond more creatively.

Conscious Experience

When we make a conscious effort to experience our environment and observe our corresponding physical and emotional sensations, we awaken more fully to each experience and to us. We can become more open and curious.

For example, compare a singer who has a limited one octave range to one who can span four octaves, including their higher, middle and lower registers. When listening to the second singer there is more for us to experience, more surprises, and more to delight in.

By increasing our sensory awareness we can also change unhappy sense memories. And we can be receptive to new sensory stimuli and consciously create fresh remembrances that fit into our new schema of how things are. When we do this, we expand our feeling abilities and experience more freedom.

The world becomes a livelier place, more colorful and responsive. We connect with full capacity to our body, our humanness and the physical world. We hear the call of our soul that thrives on our appreciation of everything around and inside us.

Conscious Viewing

When we consciously watch us, we can learn how an experience feels in our body, how easily our minds accept or don't accept what's happening. Our senses lead the way in conscious viewing. They move us to a deeper understanding of ourselves and our universe.

What's important to conscious viewing is to be fully aware of everything you're doing right now. From your breathing right down to how you're moving, to the conversation you're having and anything else that's grabbing the senses. You pay attention to the sensory information of the moment. Be aware of thoughts, images, sensations and feelings, sounds and sights. Attend to the heightened smells or tastes and how you are in the experience.

You focus on what you're doing instead of doing it automatically, and so you're really getting into each experience more actively. It may seem like a lot to ask of you and a lot of detail, but practice it. You'll find it gets easier and feels natural and enjoyable. Become more aware and more conscious of what you're doing. You'll be surprised to find out that we've tuned out to a lot of what's been going on. Some of that automatic filtering was necessary. Yet, some of what was missing from our awareness could have, for example, helped us to understand more about people. We may have had an intuitive 'sense' of what they were all about. Instead, we didn't pay attention to their body language, which held many clues to learning more about them, and we forfeited that understanding.

This time will be different. This time, we'll make a point of making our experiences more conscious by making them more sensory alive.

When you involve your senses, everything is more vivid and more convincing. Powerful messages are sent to the inner mind that this feels good. This could be anything from a massage, to soothing music, to running, to good conversation with a friend. The listening inner mind is eager to bring those feel-good experiences into play. Why? Because when you feel good it puts a certain glow or lightness to everything else you do. The more you replay them alongside what your goal or intention is, the more that direct link is set up.

Do this as though they are already taking place in the Now of your life, and they will.

> **THE EXPERIENCE THAT YOU ARE IN RIGHT NOW IS THE EXPERIENCE THAT YOU ARE IN RIGHT NOW.**

And you know it.

This is not just doubletalk. It's about being present versus sleepwalking. Truly alive to each experience with your senses or numbed and dulled to what is going on inside and around you. These are your choices. Know what is happening inside and out as you pay attention.

When you are fully paying attention and caught up in an experience, whatever aimless, rambling of thoughts that circled around in your head quiets. It doesn't always happen immediately, yet, you can teach yourself to do it. You are free to be in the moment, the totality of that experience right now. It's as though you are more present with clarity and with the use of all of your faculties.

With your senses in full gear, you are able to experience more fully, even the absence of sensation. Experience leads to greater understanding and knowledge to equip you with tools of living and creating.

Our senses lead to creation.

Sense Creation

Creating relies on some sort of visioning, a perspective. When we create a room, we consider color and light, texture, space and dimension, movement, and their relationships. We consider how they interact with our senses to provide a satisfying or meaningful, beautiful place where we can spend time and invite others.

The same is true when we invite Spirit more fully into our lives and our hearts and minds. As we expand, our creativity blossoms as well.

Sense creation uses those same elements and our eight senses to highlight a certain experience for us and to attract other experiences to us. Creating with your senses makes using what is usually automatic, not automatic at all. It includes conscious sensing. This means that we are making the effort to be aware of what's going on with our senses rather than just letting the habits take over. Once we're out of habitual sensing, we can increase our sensory know-how.

A friend of mine, who is a wonderful writer, conducts writing workshops with the use of the senses. Why is this so important? She teaches other writers to explode the use of sensory material on the page so that the reader can truly receive a more total, heightened experience of what's going on. As a result, the reader becomes more engaged in the story while their emotions are more involved as well.

Take advantage of each small experience;
They'll add up to create a life that's passionate.

Think of a young child who delights in everything, squealing at everything that's around him. All is new and full of adventure, promise and discovery. For him, everything is alive with wonder and meaning. The world is filled with sensations and sense impressions and feats that bring pleasure. It can also bring occasional pain when the stove is too hot, or walking is moving ahead and falling down.

If you are turned off to life, bathe your senses in nature or new experiences. Take moments of sensory time-out and spend time with your senses to re-discover the world of nature. Find beauty and sense aliveness anywhere, but find it.

Spend some time with a child and observe the world through child eyes. Not only his eyes but his ears and tongue, his nose, hands and feet will lead you on a trail of your own surprises.

Learn to be a kid again and look at even the most ordinary and routine parts of your life with curiosity and renewed interest. Whether you are raking leaves, baking bread, driving to work or car-pooling your kids to football practice, make each moment count.

What is there about each mundane experience that is extraordinary? Where is the novelty that stirs the soul and fires your imagination? Maybe it's something your child said, or the song of a robin that lights up your heart or calls you to wonder.

Passion and commitment are added to stir the emotional center and explode the senses into each experience for a fuller expression of self. Why are we in the body? We've landed in a body to feel and express in us and with others, our totality and connection to living and to life itself. We're here to feast with our senses on earthly delights and know love and pleasure.

What if you were never again to see a sunset, or smell the skin of a baby, or taste an orange, or pounce in the cool and tingling velvet ocean waves? Life just wouldn't be the same, would it? So live each moment as if it's the last time you'll experience it. Live each moment as if it's the last time for your senses to feel alive and life will begin to sparkle.

Each day, each moment, find ways to ignite your passion and enthusiasm. Take time to nurture the excitement you experience and to seek out those things that inspire you. When we do this over and over again, not only do we become inspired, one inspiration leads to another and we lead an impassioned life.

A friend of mine was going through a rough year and he confided in me that he had lost his passion for living. With prostate cancer, life for him had become a ceaseless series of appointments where he was pried and probed by doctors, followed by surgery, and healing. "It's as if the light blew out, and I'm standing alone in the dark," he told me. It's not that Dan didn't have a lovely family or friends; he did. He was really standing at a crossroads. No one else could change his mind or his attitude. Weeks later when I telephoned, Dan laughed heartily with me. "What happened to you?" I asked, "You seem so different."

"I made a choice to live," he told me. "My dark thoughts and fears were bringing everybody down, mostly me. So I decided not to focus on them. I found a way to see the humor and the lesson in all of it. I had to look around to see how fortunate I really am. And guess what? My granddaughter and I have taking up finger painting. And the really good news is that the doctors are optimistic about my recovery."

Dan's secret? He decided to change how he saw his life. Then he shifted his perspective. In the process of changing, he re-discovered the value and personal connections in his life. He also saw the health circumstances he had been dealt in a new way. He was back on the passion track.

If, like Dan, you're feeling numbed out about life, take moments of sensory time-out. Try bathing your senses in nature or new experiences. Rediscover the world of nature or enjoy beauty and sense-aliveness anywhere—just make sure to find it.

Okay, so what if you can't feel the sparkle of each moment and dull defines your life right now. You can change your circumstances as well as your view or perception of them.

We've already practiced ways to stimulate our familiar five senses and the mind. Now I'd also like to show you a way to expand the use of your intuitive sense.

Use this next guided imagery experience to 'dust-off' your senses and get them more vibrant than before. Whenever you feel as if your senses need to be cleared, turn to this experience and your senses will come more alive.

Activity 5: Wake Up Your Senses

Do this activity when you are in a relaxed and undisturbed time and place.

Close your eyes. Focus on your breath or count yourself down to relax. You can also tense and release your muscles to help you relax more.

Imagine that you are in a beautiful house. It's yours, although it maybe different from where you live right now. Sense that the house feels comfortable and is designed and furnished with you in mind. Wander around the first floor into the kitchen, dining room and living room areas. Sense a feeling of comfort and relaxation inside of you. You feel as if you belong here and you do.

Walk up the spiral staircase and as you reach the second floor landing you see many closed doors. Each door has a symbol on it to represent five of your senses.

At the first door, is a picture of a nose for your olfactory sense, your innate ability to smell all that's in the environment. Whenever you're ready, open the door and walk inside. You'll notice that the odors inside the room are rank and musty, as if it hasn't been cleared out in a long time. Imagine that you are cleaning out the old smelly debris and a new fresh and pleasant scent overtakes the room.

Breathe in the welcoming scents that appeal to you. As you do, you feel as if your own sense of smell is sharpening and becoming more alive. As you leave the room, you're aware of more pleasurable scents than before.

The next door has a symbol of a mouth representing your sense of taste. Enter the room and notice the total mess and disarray. Old food is stale and unappealing and no longer retains its unique smell or taste. With ease, clear the room and now sample one of your favorite dishes. Taste the spices or the sweet sensations, or whatever ingredients are inside. Enjoy the food as never before. Once the room has been cleansed, your sense of taste is more awake to lead you to more enjoyment.

Leave the room and enter the third room with a symbol for your sense of sight. Upon entering, you notice that everything inside is in clutter and blurred together. It's difficult to see and to sort out all that is there. Use cleanser and brighteners to put everything into focus and clarity. The shine and brilliance of all that's inside are wonderful. Your sense of sight is keener than before and the fog is gone.

On the fourth door is an image of two hands for your sense of touch. As you walk inside, notice a confusion of textures thrown all over from scratchy sandpaper to velvet cushions. Sort them out and touch all the different textures. Now you can really feel each one and notice the differences and nuances of each.

The fifth closed door has a picture that represents your sense of hearing. Enter now. There are so many uncomplimentary sounds that bombard your ears all at once. Once you clear this room also, something changes. The sounds are more beautiful together, harmonious like all the instruments of an orchestra playing in synch. Your sense of hearing is more defined and attentive than before, and listening is more pleasurable.

Once you exit the room, you are again in front of the spiral staircase. Notice that it spirals upward one more flight to the third floor. Go up. Here is only one room that represents your intuitive sense. It too is in need of clearing and cleansing to stimulate that sense back into life. Do so easily and begin to notice that you are becoming more aware of inner messages and feelings. You can more easily get impressions from what's around you to help you make decisions.

With your intuitive sense cleared, you can trust and rely on it more and factor in that information along with the more logical reasoning you use. Together, they can increase your understanding, judgment and accuracy. Descend the stairs. You are again on the first floor where you began. Imagine all your senses clearer and working more efficiently and reliably than before. Imagine them working beautifully alone and all together like a symphony bringing you wonderful experiences. And they will.

Take your time coming back from this relaxation. Open your eyes and stretch and yawn, slowly returning to the present and to your surroundings. Begin to use your senses with more clarity and ease. You'll find that the world around you seems brighter, clearer and perhaps more lovely than before.

Chapter Seven: Passionate Living

"We must learn to reawaken and keep ourselves awake, not by mechanical aid, but by an infinite expectation of the dawn."

Henry David Thoreau

Sense Your Passion

As you go about your life, remember to bathe all your senses in an experience that you enjoy and want to savor. In fact, get excited about all the sensory energy around you. Sometimes, I imagine that I'm a tourist in my own town just to remind myself of the ever-present opportunity to be aware. I see my world and environment with new or fresh eyes. Everything is an exciting discovery or adventure.

Life is more vivid when I do, and I pay attention to what's in my environment differently. Rather than taking it for granted, I take in everything in a new way and my environment seems novel. My interaction with it becomes a new and exhilarating experience. It can be like that for you when you attend to what's around you differently.

I have a friend who has a stream at the end of her street. When she and her family first moved to the neighborhood, they spent time at the stream. Now, five years later, she regretfully can't remember the last time that she was there. She's become numbed to the beauty around her.

Become passionate about what's around you regardless if you're living in the city, country or desert. Sense the city with all its smells of ethnic cooking steaming out of restaurants, feel the pounding heat on the asphalt and the swell of sounds and energy from the people and machines.

And the country greenery of meadows and sloping hills with berries and honeysuckle, salamanders and canapés of trees offers its own special solace and an abundant feast to your ears, eyes and nose. Just the different grass smells alone carry their own peace and ease for me. I am in awe at so many shades of green all around me and in one place. How about you? Think about the environment you live in. What stimulates you? Know what gets your senses pumping. Explore and revisit even the mundane experiences in your life. Be open to discover new sensory meaning and passion in them.

Be Passionate About Your Senses

Find passion in each one of them. You're in physical form to experience what exists on the physical plane. If you never ate your favorite food again, years later would you remember all the sensory details about it? If you can't find any joy in your life, you need to look at making changes. Call up the passion that is already inside of you as we did earlier. Awaken it and watch. Your life feels, and is, more satisfying.

Without passion, we are sleepwalkers; without passion, wonder and joy are deadened and we are only a whisper of our true self.

There are so many natural sensory treasures that we take for granted. If we tune into them more fully, they will positively affect our moods, thoughts and wellness.

So trust yourself. Go on an intimate journey to find your passion in living and to create excitement with each experience. Passion can be uplifting and inspiring and may help you achieve what you never dreamed possible. At the soul level, at the core of you, is where this enthusiasm lives.

Awaken to Passion

Vicki, a 45-year-old client of mine, said she was unable to feel passion in her life. She knew she was a passionate person and remembered when she used to feel excited and be engaged about life. Yet now she was physically and mentally exhausted and lacking any real feeling. Life was dull and drab. She felt like she was just going through the motions. Vicki didn't know how to get off her life's mechanical merry-go-round. Her job as a medical secretary paid the bills...well, just barely. And because of cutbacks and layoffs her duties had increased.

She was working longer and longer hours but her pay stayed the same. In her time off, all she did was catch up on sleep so she could go to work and do it all over again. Any thrill that life once gave her had been sucked dry by the monotonous routine. She had left her dreams of running a company and teaching somewhere back in her childhood. She said she couldn't resurrect them. Anyway, she was too tired to try.

In our sessions, we began to play a game to stir the passions of her senses. She identified her passions and then chose one passion and flooded it with awareness, enthusiasm and sensory amplification. As Vicki's senses rekindled, her passions rolled over into other moments. As Vicki fed her senses, she felt more refreshed. She decided she had to make a choice: find some other work that she could feel better about, or figure out some way to put the oomph back into her job.

Realizing that her job was the culprit that made her life feel so dry and brittle was easy. Doing something about it was the challenge Vicki faced. When she mustered the courage to leave, she found a job in a smaller office. There, she felt appreciated by her manager and was able to be appreciative of life's small pleasures. Vicki was soon able to show off her own management skills. More responsibility was turned over to her by her manager who recognized that she was a take-charge person. She trained new hires by acclimating them to the company and company policy.

Passionate Living

What does it mean to live passionately? It means living with a sense of excitement—with the feeling that life has meaning and color, purpose and joy. Passion gives us the energy and gusto to create and dream, even when we walk through times of turmoil and difficulty. Not every step of the way is going to be rose-colored. It's unrealistic to think that's so when reaching for a goal, designing or re-designing a life plan.

In those challenging moments, it's important to keep steadfast on your goal or vision and continue to remember why you're passionate about it. Let the passion for that dream be ever-present and be the constant reminder of why you are spending long hours at the computer, or calling up prospective clients, or whatever task you are completing.

Grow Your Passion

However, passion doesn't just happen; it grows from the inside out. The blueprint for creating it is as unique as a fingerprint. What thrills you is different from what thrills me, which is different from what excites your family and friends. Only you know what stimulates you and lets your passion loose. I urge you to find what gets your juices flowing and spend some significant time doing it.

What makes you come alive? Is it massaging scented oils into your lover's naked skin? Does skiing down a steep snowy slope in Vermont enliven you? Or do you find your pleasure by crushing garlic and fresh basil as you try-out a new pasta recipe to entice your family?

I have learned to find and create passion in life's little pleasures. Watching and participating in the changing seasons while really engaging my senses make my passion for life expand. I delight in breathing in the new cherry blossom scents in springtime and watching buds peek out on the trees as I wait expectantly for them to bloom. My enthusiasm for life grows when I write, teach and touch the hearts and minds of others.

Passion surges as I stroke my Siamese cat and she rolls over, exposing her soft furry belly to my touch. Her purr, warmth and vulnerability and the amazing trust that she has in me, all plunge me into passion. Even an organic dark chocolate truffle given to me by my sister on her last visit to my home in New Jersey can thrill me. As it melts on my tongue, its sweetness and the bond between us sisters, regardless of our differences, open me up. My passion is also fired up during lively conversations where I share my ideas and ideals with close friends.

Keep Passion Alive

Is passion alive in your life? It may have dimmed if you are spending too much time doing activities that you don't want to do. And, if you're in places you really don't want to be, as many of us are these days. What if you're feeling bogged down by life? Or, if every day is lived out of habit and grind without feeling any real enthusiasm. Maybe your job is not exciting to you though you're not yet ready to change it.

Maybe you feel stuck in a marriage that has lost its color and feels drab and lackluster. I'm not suggesting to everyone that you quit your job or wring out your marriage in divorce court. Staying where you are can be fine when you discover and create moments that excite you. Maybe your hobbies fire you up, or the time you spend working out at the gym, or bicycling down a wooded path. Or maybe it's those special moments with your children or grandchildren that are golden.

Are you doing what you're doing most of the time because you have to? Do your relationships drain you and leave you lacking? Do you feel restless and dissatisfied? If you answer yes to these questions then you need to look at your life. Re-think what's important to you. By recognizing the stirrings of your heart and the ideas, activities and feelings that make your imagination leap, you can live with more enjoyment. You'll reach your goals more easily, too. Loving what you're doing will make the task feel lighter.

Identify Your Passions

No matter what your direction is and what goals you are choosing to create in your life, create them with a sense of passion. Passion fuels them and generates the enthusiasm and the sense of urgency in bringing those goals to you. If you're not excited about what you're doing, beware. That's the message you're communicating to your mind.

Remember that your feelings are important in how the Law of Attraction works. Passion can be just the magnet to convey not only to you, but to the Universe, that what you want in your life also feels good and is worthwhile. If you are half-hearted and really not too thrilled about what you're about to create, then your subconscious thinks why bother.

To stir up the passion in your life, you first have to identify what your passions are. What are you really passionate about? Take the time, right now, with the activities in this chapter to create a list of your passions. They can be related to work such as organizing, contact with people or research. Or they can be about the activities that you love to do such as scuba diving, sailing, gourmet cooking or hanging out with your spouse and kids.

After you've finished writing down your list of passions, you are ready to review what's there. Now, examine your list. Is there an activity that you haven't squeezed into your schedule? Make some room for it now. Is it a friend you feel good with when you share and laugh together? Call up that friend. Don't put positive experiences on the back burner; they need to stay active in your life. Feeling good is what it's all about, not suffering.

You owe it to yourself to allow good feelings and experiences into your life with more frequency. When you choose passion, life seems more alive and meaningful. Don't wait to include what's on your passion list in your life. You deserve to experience it now and to create the time for your passions.

Live Passionately

I once worked with a client named Jeremy. He was a successful accountant, a loving parent and a loving husband. When he came into my office, he confided that he was unhappy. He also had a heart condition that he was being medically treated for. Jeremy just couldn't account for the sadness he was feeling and didn't know where to turn. To him, being depressed didn't make any sense. His life was going well by social standards; he had a devoted family, financial success, friends he treasured. Since everything seemed to be fine, he didn't understand why he felt the way he did—downright lousy and blah.

His work was suffering and his relationship with his wife was bending under the strain of his discomfort and unhappiness. Jeremy felt he couldn't continue his life in the same way. He began to question the meaning of his life and the choices he had made. As he talked, it made sense to me that both Jeremy's heart and spirit were suffering under the weight of not living his heart's desires.

Jeremy felt guilty and uncomfortable about his feelings and tried to deny they were real. He even apologized, which signaled to me that something wasn't right. His feelings embarrassed him and he didn't think he should have them. He felt they were selfish and foolish and didn't fit with the success that he had in his life.

"Why should you apologize for how you're feeling?" I questioned. He didn't know but still was uncomfortable. To Jeremy, everything was going just how it was supposed to. By all standards, his life was on track. But even though it didn't feel like enough, he thought he was unreasonable to expect more. Yet deep down inside, Jeremy had always wanted to be a musician.

When he was younger, he played piano. Jeremy loved to run his fingers along the keys to hear all the different sound combinations possible. Later on, he taught himself acoustic guitar. He and his friends formed a band and played at local gatherings. As Jeremy told me the story of his musical past, the look on his face changed; he became more animated.

His voice was richer, like it came from a different place inside of him.

Jeremy's early dreams of being a musician were wrenched away from him when his father died when Jeremy was sixteen. At that point, his life changed dramatically. He switched his focus to figuring out how to make money. Only then could he help support his mom and two younger sisters and fund his college education. He believed he had to be "the man" and that he had to be responsible.

This belief was reinforced by his mother. Out of her own fear and need to have Jeremy help out at home, she told him he was now "the man of the house" and needed to behave responsibly. During his last year of high school, Jeremy studied hard and worked long hours at night at a grocery store. He was tired but pushed on, never wanting to disappoint his mother or leave his sisters in a lurch.

At college when Jerry met Marie and fell in love with her, he vowed to himself that he'd never leave his future wife and family in a financial hole. He spent the next eighteen years focusing on making money. He was consumed with making sure that they would always have what he didn't—a financial safety net. Jeremy felt proud that he had been able to do just that for his family. Now he had the money, the investments and the planned-out retirement; however, his emptiness had increased.

"Do you own a piano?" I asked.

"No, my two boys are into soccer, football, basketball and girls."

"Why don't you get one?"

"They won't play."

"They don't have to play," I told him. "The piano is for you. You can play!"

Jeremy looked at me and said nothing. Within a month, he bought a piano and now plays whenever he can. In fact, he's a hit at family reunions. Jeremy regained his joy when he re-introduced music into his life. As a gifted musician, his soul and soul searching had prodded him not to deny something that was truly important to him.

Embracing music and appreciating his own musical talent made him feel more alive and genuine. Music was as necessary to him as were the other important areas of his life. Ignoring it meant denying who he was. With music back in his life, Jerry regained his enthusiasm and felt that his life was complete. In addition to all the wonderful people and abundance, Jeremy now had the music that fed his spirit.

Passion Recall

You can also recall a passion memory and replay it with as much detail and pleasure, so that you can re-experience those feelings and stir up those passions in the present moment. Indirectly, by doing this, your past passion can influence you right now.

Focus on a specific time when you were living your passion. Remember the day, the weather, the other people and the scenery (indoors or outdoors). Recall what was said and remember minute details if you can, even down to what you were wearing. What made the day or event so special in your mind?

Now remember to also involve your senses in this memory experience (include your thoughts and feelings). Pay attention to the sights, smell, tastes, textures and sounds, bringing them into your awareness right now. Once you've done that, pump up your senses even more. Exaggerate feeling good and exaggerate all the sensory information and experiences that were present. By pumping up your senses, you are creating those feelings with the ability for them to come back to you again in new ways.

I recently read about the potential health benefits of the scent of peppermint. It positively impacts cognitive behavior such as motivation and can influence the physical performance of athletes. Scientists found that by introducing peppermint, the threshold of pain increased for the subjects. Smells, like peppermint, may offer relief from physical pain that so many people suffer from. And that's not all. Continued research in sensory enhancement may show us more possibilities for health enhancement as well.

What does this mean for you? Be your own voyager into the sensory world to enrich your experiences. Experiment by filtering out one sense at a time; turn up one sense while turning down the volume or intensity of the other senses.

Immediately your senses will be sharpened and you'll find yourself attending to more detail and more information with each sense. Over time and with practice, your senses will develop even more. The information you will receive from each sense will expand, making your experience on earth and in your body and mind fuller and more alive.

We've heard the expression, "You are what you think". Our thoughts create our reality for us. What we pay attention to, and focus on with our thoughts is bound to be in our lives. Yet there's more. Not only are you what you think about. You are also what you feel. Thoughts and feelings affect your reality.

Oh That Powerful Feeling

Our feelings and emotions are powerhouses. They carry so much energy and can have us reeling from fear or somersaulting with excitement. Just as with your thoughts; you do have a choice here. Choose the emotions and feelings that are satisfying.

You can wake up feeling grumpy and angry at your spouse and the world for the rote job you go to every weekday, or because the dog needs to go out and it's 3:00 am and you only fell asleep a couple of hours ago. Or you can change that first emotional response you have that wants to take you down a negative mudslide.

Get Satisfaction

How? You can make something else happen instead. Send out feelings of satisfaction. Find something, anything in your immediate environment that gives you that warm, good feeling like holding your child, snuggling with your partner, a pat on the back from your boss, a sale.

Whatever it is, and for each of us that emotional feel-good experience is different. You can make those emotions serve you consciously. I'm not suggesting that you ignore what you feel and pretend you don't feel uncomfortable or annoyed or jealous. Feel all those feelings. And then with awareness, change them.

As with your thoughts, it is important that you know what you're feeling and experiencing so that you can take charge of those feelings. Then you can consciously create new feelings that vibrate more in the frequency of joy or well-being.

If there's nothing in your home or work area to turn on those feelings and you still feel down, recall an event that was pleasing to you. In recall, remember to recreate those same feelings as best you can over and over, until your mood and vibration shift. You'll know when that is. You're calmer and less overwhelmed, and is it possible you're even smiling?

If it feels like you're making it up, that's okay. Act as though you're playing the part of your life! You are. Once these comfortable feelings are familiar and easy for you to call up in a few moments, you will be able to create emotions that can bring you the results you seek. You will feel better as you do so.

Activity 6A: My Passion List

Jot down ten or more items that you are passionate about. List ten items that are already in your life now as well as those that are not in your life yet. Just make sure that you feel passionate about whatever they are.

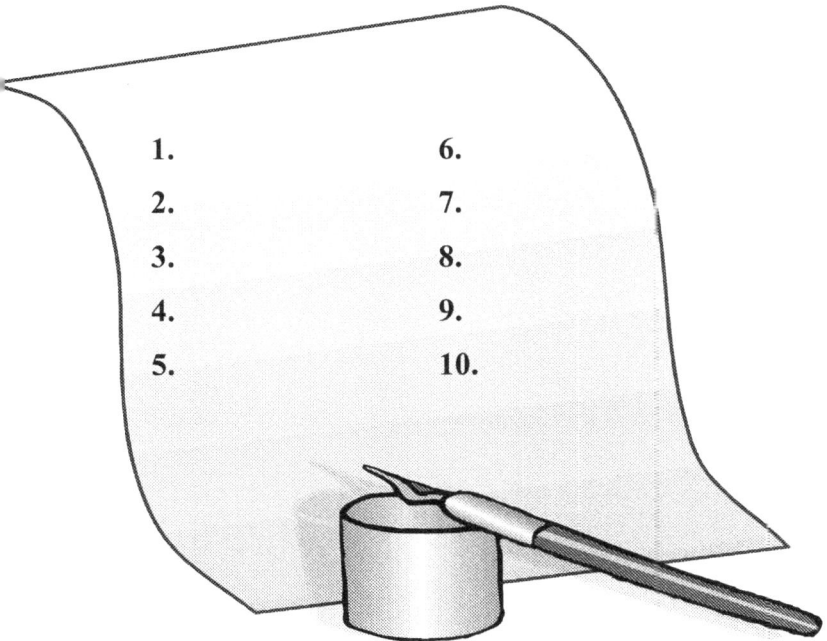

1.   6.

2.   7.

3.   8.

4.   9.

5.   10.

Activity 6B: Satisfaction Now

❖ What are you feeling right now? Pick something
   that feels good in your environment or your life to
   pay attention to.

❖ Get happy about that something as you focus and
   think more about it.

❖ Add other pleasant sense information to it like a
   favorite scent, colors that relax and appeal to you.
   Include as many senses as you can.

❖ Turn your senses up even higher.

❖ Use your imagination and make it all feel really
   real.

Chapter Eight: Become a Sensory Magnet

"We don't see things as they are; we see them as we are."

Anais Nin

Life Design

You have the opportunity to redesign and remodel your life. You can fashion, design, invent and re-invent your life and you. Your intentions are powerful in making your choices really happen. What you think and repeat to you also holds power.

In manifesting, belief must be present. It doesn't really matter what the physical reality looks like at the moment. You can be living in a trailer, or a teepee with visions of owning a colonial home. The chance of getting that home is slim if you don't think you'll get close to your vision. And, just as unlikely if your beliefs are stuck on what you have now. Or, if your beliefs are stuck on what you don't have.

Release Limitation

The limitations in your life right now don't have to remain there forever. How do you breathe life into the vision or thought of what you'd like? Believe you can shift your reality, and you will.

It's easy to get things going when what you presently have is not far off from the mark. When you have to stretch your belief because what you choose hasn't shown up in your life, and looks like it never will, that's the challenge. It's only a challenge, not impossible.

The reason we're challenged is because we've never really believed that something so precious could, would or should be a part of our life. Deep down, we don't believe we can get it. This belief keeps going strong because everything that we manifest is in keeping with that belief. The message is that it's just not possible.

The energy and vibration that we send out matches that message that it isn't possible. And we're not surprised when we don't get it. You can change all that right now with so much as a different thought, belief or feeling. Together they work more powerfully.

Sense Aliveness

So how do we change what is lacking? How can we alter our lives into something else?

Again, it is with the senses. Only this time, we use our senses with consciousness. We weave sensory impressions and sense aliveness that are favorable to us. We also change our old stories, history and responses to the situations and outcomes that we choose. Mentally, we have the chance to do it over, but differently. This time we reenact the moment to our advantage.

We use our senses as tools, arms, tongues, ears, nostrils, eyes, bodies and feelings to arouse them into awakening. New scripts are crafted that affect our present and impact the future with the aliveness of the senses at the helm.

Fire up Your Senses

With conscious awareness, we'll use our senses as bait. We will make each experience meaningful, interesting and attractive enough to convince our filters to commit the experience, thought and feeling to long-term memory. Otherwise, our filters can block it, but not if it's loaded with so much appeal for us. With the senses fired up, the experiences live on long remembered. And we can activate them at will.

Why do we do this? We already know what feels good to us because at some point we really had those feelings and senses. Now we are going to use those same feel-good experiences and attach them to what we expect, and choose to make real in our lives.

Activity 7: Sensory Creation

1. Write down something you want to bring
    into your life and reality right now. It's time
    to put it out there and make it real for you to
    see. It's time to openly ask for what you
    desire.

2. Create vivid pictures and images, feelings along with
    the use of all your other seven senses. Pump them up!

3. Sense the different scenes and stories that you make up
    on a screen in your mind (eyes opened or shut)
    happening right now.

4. Sense you enjoying these experiences and this outcome
    to the hilt.

After all, here it is. And you, master creator that you are,
created it. So make the most of it and include other people
you care about in the scenes you create. Believe it's here
without a shred of fear or doubt. Know it and know it
without question, doubt or waver. Expect it right now.

Chapter Nine: Sense Appreciation

"If we could see the miracle of a single flower clearly, our whole life would change."

Buddha

Appreciation

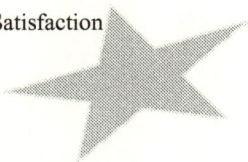

When was the last time you looked around you in your home, really looked, or in your garden and just breathed in everything – the cooking smells, the fragrant smells of your garden or the lawn freshly mowed?

How recently have you just looked over at your kids playing, or your spouse sleeping? You stopped whatever you were doing at that moment and listened to the laughter or the quiet breathing. And you just took it in, all of it, and felt an inner smile. This is appreciation.

Appreciation is an approach to life and everything that's in it from a snowstorm to warm peach pie. We can focus only on the hazards of driving in the snow and the road delays, or we can also recognize the beauty of each snow crystal, the fun activities like skiing and making snowmen that people engage in and how the moisture supports plant and animal life.

The way each of us experiences life is different and based on our individual and personal perceptions. Our senses play a significant role in all of this. They add special meaning to each situation and can rely on former sense-memories or impressions.

Every experience is new; and will never be the same again. Even if an event is repeated, it's not the same as before. Think about it. Every moment is unlike any other. Why? The sensations are different, the smells, tastes, sounds and what you are seeing, touching, or feeling is not the same as before. What a gift to realize the precious value of each moment, each experience, knowing that it will never come around in the same way.

You have an opportunity to take it all in, pay attention to all the sensations as fully as you can, once you realize this fact. I recommend that you spend some time and take in what usually seems mundane and recognize its significance.

You're outside, standing under a canapé, waiting for a friend who's late. It's raining and while you're waiting, your thoughts drift to, "Where is he?" and "I wish it wasn't so wet and rainy. My good shoes are all soaked." These thoughts really have no purpose or direction. They are part of the self-talk, the doubts, and mindless annoyances that we engage in.

You have a choice here. Rather than focus on the negative, the irritation of your friend's lateness, you can attend to the experience of you waiting in the rain and take in all of your surroundings. Listen to the sound of the rain, each individual droplet that contributes to the overall experience of rain.

Listen to the quality of the sound as the rain gets heavier and then lighter; the sound is different. Watch the rain drops as they fall on the cement and see the puddles forming in some places, rolling in others. Smell the air. Feel how dense it is during a rain shower and how it gets lighter as the rain tapers off as though the earth has been cleansed.

What you are doing is appreciating life in the moment and taking all of it in with your senses and perceptions. You are aware of everything around you; your awareness is heightened as you fully participate in the moment. Rain will never be the same for you again.

Finding the joy in the moment is in your sensory reach. Know it with each sense experience you have.

I remember an experience that happened some time ago. It was early April and the cold winter winds and bone-chilling damp still lingered. The days were gray and dreary. Where was spring hiding? I was in a sleepy-funk and weary of it all; my thoughts turned to the dismal and dark.

As I was about to be taken for a spin by my own mind, weaving groaning tales of gloom, I stopped and looked at my options. If I rode the wave of this type of thinking,   I was headed for more doom and gloom. I certainly didn't need that in my life right now—if ever.

So I changed course and lassoed in my thoughts and put my beliefs into action. I turned to my senses for the explosion. The hiss of the wind in the frosted-over trees, mingled with a Wyndam Hill CD playing in the background, pulled me into the moment. The spice of ginger tea steeping in the kitchen wafted upstairs. I paused in the hallway and just stretched my body, appreciating the pleasure of moving and the freedom of my muscles in even the smallest movements.

Life and movement and energy were all around when I consciously tuned into my senses. I was captive to the moment and a quiet joy simmering. In those few moments, my attention shifted to my senses and information of a different kind. Pleasing sensations and associations took over and my thoughts changed. I felt better and the day ahead had more appeal than before. The negative thoughts were upstaged and I was in charge. My senses were responsible for the distraction.

Appreciation is a sure-fire way to get the vibrations in motion for what it is you're choosing to bring into your life.

When you use it and it works, you'll think magic has just been set free. It's not magic at all. You are working with that unstoppable Law of Attraction. You can use appreciation more consciously for your goals and dreams.

Activity 8: Appreciate Your World

Make a list of what you appreciate in your life right now. Add to it often.

1.   6.

2.   7.

3.   8.

4.   9.

5.   10.

Choose an item from the list and pump up your sense feelings about it even more to increase your appreciation. Do this with as many items as you can on your list and watch your appreciation grow exponentially.

Chapter Ten: Self Appreciation

"...I think the real miracle is not to walk either on water or thin air but to walk on earth.

Every day we are engaged in a miracle we don't even recognize: a blue sky, white clouds, green leaves, black, curious eyes of a child — our own two eyes. All is a miracle."

Thich Nhat Hanh

Internal Messages

Okay, so you think that you feel pretty good about yourself. But somehow, you've been listening to those automatically programmed messages in your head that say otherwise. It's not unusual to have those old tapes rewind over and over. They pipe into your head thoughts and feelings, messages that you don't care to hear anymore.

You don't have to listen. You can replace the old tapes with new tapes that tell you something different and more self-affirming; you can do it right now. Self appreciation is the best remedy for ongoing self-critical tapes that play on in our minds. The critical automatic talk plants seeds of doubts, imperfections, and unworthiness. No longer must you be a slave to them and obey their messages. Now you can plant seeds that affirm you and affirm your life!

Self-Acceptance

No, it's not bragging or being so full of yourself that others think your ego is too large for your head and body. It's about accepting you and where you are right now, even if you're not exactly where you want to be. Most likely, you still have goals and dreams that are emerging or haven't even been jumpstarted. That's fine and human, so don't get out of whack about it. Instead, do find ways to recognize your worth and value without a certain yearly income, job or relationship.

Finding value in you, no matter what, is no small task.
You have to be fair and caring to you and not holdback what you need. To create what's been missing, you need to be gentle and forgiving of you. You won't do it by beating yourself up, and if by chance you do, it won't be a hearty victory because your heart won't believe you.

Practicing self-acceptance

To observe yourself accurately, you have to let go of the need to be "perfect" and learn to practice accepting who you are right now. You do this regardless of what you have or have not done in the past. Practicing self-acceptance helps you let go of self-criticism and the "should haves" that often follow.

In self-acceptance, we allow for our human imperfections. We take responsibility for the shadowy, dark sides of ourselves—the parts we avoid and hide from. These aspects of our personalities have tremendous power. When we accept ourselves and our situation with compassion, it's easier to make changes if we choose to do so.

The practice of self-acceptance may feel difficult at first. Our society teaches us to strive to be perfect. Many of us have become masters at "beating up" on ourselves. Yet, when we judge ourselves unfavorably, we create more uncomfortable feelings about us. We may think this will motivate us, but if it does, it does so only for a short time.

Then it's back to flogging ourselves and deflating our own egos. This kind of behavior saps our energy—energy that might have been used to make constructive changes in our lives.

Release the Struggle

By accepting where and who we are right now and letting go of our need to be someone we're not, we also release the struggle. Life becomes a little easier. New possibilities can now come into being that couldn't show up when we were battling ourselves.

It's not always pleasant to look at how far we've fallen or the roles we play that keep us from being whole. When I sprained my ankle, my reaction to it is a perfect example. Initially, after twisting it, my attitude toward my seemingly ankle-centered life was sullen and grumpy. I grumbled about my fate and blamed everything for my misfortune. I felt oh-so-sorry for myself and dwelled on my calamity. The victim role was played out with an Oscar-winning performance as I sat around feeling limited. I tried to push myself to resume my activities at the hectic pace I had become used to. My annoyance sprung up whenever I had to cancel some appointments.

My impatience glared at me like a red flag! "Pay attention," it screamed! What did I need to understand? I should have realized I couldn't continue to push myself without giving my ankle time to heal. Instead, my impatience and rushing about interfered with the healing process. Had I been paying attention, I would have realized that rushing and impatience had led to my injury in the first place.

All my pushing didn't change anything. The ankle took more time to heal. My mental and emotional malaise grew stronger and uglier. The longer I resisted slowing down and taking care of myself, the more my ankle swelled. When I pushed myself to carry on with my activities and exercises, at the same feverish rate, my ankle rebelled. Inflammation and pain increased. Movement was downright uncomfortable and I was trapped in a vicious cycle of my own creation.

Of course, not accepting my situation and being so hard on myself only caused me to experience more friction. I was more irritable and impatient with loved ones and lashed out at them. After the cutting words, I felt badly for my outburst. I discovered that I wasn't only being hard on myself but on others as well. Figuring out what I was doing took a while.

Eventually, I realized I had to give in and accept that my reaction—and it definitely was a wild reaction to what happened—was my choice. So I was handed lemons—I could work with lemons! That realization, that acceptance, was the starting point to my emotional and physical healing.

Self-acceptance can also be the beginning of something new and special for you. Without the struggle and the drama that we create by trying to be so perfect, we just realize it isn't so. Here you are and, amazingly, you're fine and you were fine all the time.

Self Worth

What's it worth to you? A great deal and you don't have to take a backseat to feeling good. Instead, you recognize that you deserve to have good and abundance in your life. It's not just a fairy tale to soothe young children. Feeling good about you, despite your mistakes and shortcomings, is to know that you are good enough and fine the way you are.

It doesn't discount the self-improvements you may want to make. Who doesn't want to strive to be all that she can be? While you're striving, you don't hesitate. You don't doubt your worth and your ability to be a powerful life creator, because you are—always. The time to believe and act on that information and on your worthiness is right now.

Appreciate You

Some time ago, I received a card from a dear friend that really made a difference in my life. Fifteen years later, I still have that card and the message is as valuable now as it was then.

The card reads: **You are the Celebration.**

Not only are you the celebration of your own life and cause for that celebration of you all the time, you're the miracle as well. You may not regard you in this way—but why not? Your abilities to sense, love, laugh, think, dream and imagine are outstanding. You are continuously capable of growing and learning and becoming more of whom you are—becoming all that you want to be.

In all of my seminars and classes, I remind people to celebrate the wonder and miracle of who they are. Just the fact that we are thinking, feeling, breathing, moving beings is truly amazing. When was the last time you celebrated yourself? Do so now. Remind yourself of your goodness. Find something that you did that you feel good about. And rejoice in the wonder of who you are.

What is it like to regard you as a living, breathing, creating conscious miracle with the miraculous ability to change your life? Can you imagine believing and acting on that information every single day that you're alive?

No matter what obstacles appear or fears mount, you can view you as able and worthy of receiving life's bounty. And you are armed with the tools and belief to attract it. You feel strong and open, energized, loving and optimistic and ready to tackle any challenge. At the same time, you expect and welcome the new conscious choices that you are making right now. You wait expectantly for them, and they do appear.

So rather than giving in to negative or defeating self-talk, create ways to sing your praises and feel your goodness. How else will you recognize your own uniqueness and worth? Is it keeping a journal to track all of your good deeds? Or, can you praise you often and be supportive and forgiving when you've made a mistake? Finding ways to nurture and respect you and demonstrate your own importance to you are revealing and necessary. They are messages that say you value you. When you repeatedly engage in actions that are self-supportive and self-loving, those messages become stronger and more believable.

Create ways to appreciate you every day. And while you're at it, do the same for others. I guarantee you'll feel good. Not only will you be doing a service, the other person will feel good too. You'll also be attracting those feelings more into your life and into the life of your friend.

My Life Canvas

Today, here and now, we are the ones spinning dreams onto our canvases of life and deciding with our hearts and our minds what lands on the life canvas. The choice is a conscious one and we make it known quietly and aloud. We activate the choice when we enliven our senses.

With our senses, we are fully present in the moment, taking in stimuli that are fragrant, flavorful, hot, harmonious, colorful or stark. We take in life in all its hues and imprints. We feel more deeply and remember with the senses. Turn them up a notch. Do it consciously and willingly because it adds vibrancy to what you know and what you are learning.

Breathe in the scent of a loved one, feel the heat and the closeness on a New York subway. Or, rub your cheek against a fragrant rose petal and inhale. A poem, a song lifts us and touches our heartstrings, giving expression to the nuances and shades of feelings we have.

With your imagination, the soul finds its outward expression in your life. With your senses, the soul sings inwardly and outwardly and brings you closer to experiencing the special beauty and wonder of being alive.

Dream your dreams and awaken to your own Wonderland in which you shimmer and shine. Believe in you and appreciate you. Appreciate all the possibilities that you can bring to you and your world.

"This world, after all our science and sciences, is still a miracle; wonderful, inscrutable, magical and more, to whosoever will think of it."

Thomas Carlyle

Activity 9A: The Wonder of You

You can do this activity while sitting, walking or lying down, eyes open or closed, depending on where you are.

Just imagine that you are in a beautiful place that supports you and feels safe and loving, indoors or outside, somewhere you feel good about you.

Recall a proud time or event for you, no matter how long ago it happened or how current it is. What matters is that you choose a time and experience when you felt good about you and bring it into this moment.

Imagine you feeling comfortable and relaxed and glowing with a sense of pride and satisfaction in you. Expand that feeling even more and make the feeling really large. Amplify it as much as you can.

Recall all the information pouring in that enhances how you feel. And stay there as long as you can. Now, if you can't recall such a time, make up a time and memory that conjure a proud and wonderful feeling about you. And this time, do it with amplification.

Sense you now, in a present or future situation. Sense your feelings regarding you and your worth pumped up so that your joy and sense of self are enhanced.

Engage all your senses. Pay attention to what's happening with them to make the feelings you have about you more believable, memorable and repeatable.

Enjoy you and see you strong, loving and worthy. See you gazing right back at you, enjoying and basking in the favorable attention, and why not? You deserve every bit of it. And the best news is that you're bringing it to you.

Activity 9 B: I Am a Shining Star

Jot down all the reasons, large or small, why you are a shining star in your life and in the lives of others, especially those you care for. You can even ask them how you're special to them. What they say can be an eye–opener.

1. _____   6. _____

2. _____   7. _____

3. _____   8. _____

4. _____   9. _____

5. _____   10. _____

Think about the ways in which you shine right now and also write down how you intend to shine even more brightly in the future.

References

Ackerman, Diane. A Natural History of the Senses. New York: Vintage Books, 1990.

Alexander, F.M. The Use of the Self. Long Beach, CA: Centerline Press, 1985.

Byrne, Rhonda. The Secret. New York: Atria Books, 2006.

Campell, Joseph. The Mythic Image. Bollingen Series C. Princeton: University Press, 1974.

Card, Scott, Orson. Children of the Mind. New York: Tor, 1996.

Chopra, Deepak. How to Know God: The Soul's Journey into the Mystery of Mysteries. New York: Three Rivers Press, 2001.

Crosette, Barbara. "A Thai Monk Unlocks Song in the Earth." The New York Times, December 30, 1987.
Dyer, Wayne. The Power of Intention. California: Hay House, 2004.

Dyer, Wayne. There's a Spiritual Solution to Every Problem. New York: Harper Collins, 2001.

Emoto, Masaru. The Hidden Messages in Water. Oregon: Beyond Words Publishing, 2004.

Ford, Debbie. The Dark Side of the Light Chasers. New York: Riverhead Books, 1998.

Grof, Stanislav. The Holotropic Mind. New York: HarperCollins, 1993.

Hillman, James. The Soul's Code. New York: Random House, 1996.

Jung, C. G., Synchronicity, An Acausal Connecting Principle. Bollingen Series Princeton University Press: 1969.

McTaggart, Lynne. The Field: The Quest for the Secret Force of the Universe. New York: Harper Collins, 2002.

Michalko, Michael. Cracking Creativity: The Secrets of Creative Genius. Ten Speed Press: Berkley, CA, 2001.

Moore, Thomas. Care of the Soul. HarperCollins Pub.: New York, 1992.

Naparstek, Belleruth. Your Sixth Sense: Unlucking your Psychic Potential. HarperCollins Pub.: New York, NY, 1997.

Roach, Michael. The Tibetan book of yoga: ancient Buddhist teachings on the path and practice of yoga. Doubleday: New York, NY, 2004.

Tiller, William A. Science and Human transformation: Subtle Energies, Intentionality and Consciousness. Walnut Creek, CA: Pavior Publishing, 1997.

Sheldrake, Matthew and Rupert. Natural Grace: Dialogues on Creation, Darkness, and the Soul in Spirituality and Science. New York: Doubleday, 1996

Whyte, David. The Heart Arouses. Poetry and the Preservation of the Soul in Corporate America. New York: Doubleday, 1994.

Wilber, Ken. A Brief History of Everything. Boston: Shambhala, 1996.

Wilber, Ken. Eye to Eye: The Quest for the New Paradigm. Boston: Shambhala, 1996.

Wolf, Fred Alan. Mind into Matter: A New Alchemy of Science and Spirit. New Hampshire: Moment Point Press, 2000.

Zukav, Gary. The Heart of the Soul. New York: Simon & Schuster, 2001.

Zukav, Gary. The Seat of the Soul. New York: Simon & Schuster, 1989.

About The Author:

Known to audiences throughout the world as the 'Success Doc", Dr. Jo Anne White is an author, international speaker, life coach and therapist. Her relationship advice has been sought after by live radio and television audiences such as CN8 and NBC.

For over twenty years, Dr. White has helped thousands of men and women overcome personal and professional challenges and find direction and success in their lives. She has helped couples find more relationship satisfaction.

Dr. White is a professional motivational and keynote speaker. She has been featured in magazines and newspapers throughout the United States and Canada some of which include Match.com, House and Garden, Woman's World and WebMD.

You are invited to check out more books, as well as other products and seminars developed by Dr. White.

To Contact Dr. Jo Anne White directly:

Call **1-877-Doc White or Write:**

PO Box 176

Haddonfield, NJ

08033

Remember Doc White is available for private and confidential consultations.

Please check out Dr. White's other books, CD's and products designed with you in mind.

www.docwhite.org

Visit: http://www.drjoannewhite.com/jawstore.html   for more life affirming products and information.

Visit: www.docwhite.org to read more inspirational articles and news

Also by Doc White:

Books:

How to Love: Secrets to Lasting Relationships

Making Sense: Pump up the Pleasure in Your Life with Perception

Surviving a Break-up: Your Guide to Recovery

Breaking Up: Letting Go with Grace

Living without Fear

CD's & Programs:

Focus on Success

Journey into Relaxation

Total Sense® Life Success Programs, CD's and Seminars

www.docwhite.org